AGRICULTURE

▶ Energy From Plants?

▶ Drones on the Farm

▶ GMO Controversy in the Sea

Agriculture

Energy

Entertainment Industry

Environment & Sustainability

Forensics

Information Technology

Medicine and Health Care

Space Science

Transportation

War and the Military

AGRICULTURE

By John Perritano

MASON CREST

Mason Crest
450 Parkway Drive, Suite D
Broomall, PA 19008
www.masoncrest.com

Printed and bound in the United States of America.

First printing
9 8 7 6 5 4 3 2 1

Series ISBN: 978-1-4222-3587-4
ISBN: 978-1-4222-3588-1
ebook ISBN: 978-1-4222-8289-2

Produced by Shoreline Publishing Group
Designer: Tom Carling, Carling Design Inc.
Production: Sandy Gordon
www.shorelinepublishing.com

Front cover photos: boarding1now/Dreamstime tl; Scott Griessel/Dreamstime tr; AquaBounty Technologies b.

Library of Congress Cataloging-in-Publication Data

Names: Perritano, John, author.
Title: Agriculture / by John Perritano.
Other titles: STEM in current events.
Description: Broomall, PA : Mason Crest, [2017] | Series: STEM in current
   events | Includes index.
Identifiers: LCCN 2016004741| ISBN 9781422235881 (hardback) | ISBN
   9781422235874 (series) | ISBN 9781422282892 (ebook)
Subjects: LCSH: Agriculture--Juvenile literature. | Agricultural
   innovations--Juvenile literature. | Agricultural mathematics--Juvenile
   literature.
Classification: LCC S493 .P467 2017 | DDC 630--dc23
LC record available at http://lccn.loc.gov/2016004741

Contents

Key Icons to Look For

Words to Understand: These words with their easy-to-understand definitions will increase the reader's understanding of the text, while building vocabulary skills.

Sidebars: This boxed material within the main text allows readers to build knowledge, gain insights, explore possibilities, and broaden their perspectives by weaving together additional information to provide realistic and holistic perspectives.

Educational Videos: Readers can view videos by scanning our QR codes, providing them with additional educational content to supplement the text. Examples include news coverage, moments in history, speeches, iconic sports moments, and much more!

Text-Dependent Questions: These questions send the reader back to the text for more careful attention to the evidence presented here.

Research Projects: Readers are pointed toward areas of further inquiry connected to each chapter. Suggestions are provided for projects that encourage deeper research and analysis.

Series Glossary of Key Terms: This back-of-the-book glossary contains terminology used throughout this series. Words found here increase the reader's ability to read and comprehend higher-level books and articles in this field.

 Biologists around the country are seeking answers to the problem of the disappearing honeybees. The insects play a vital role in producing food and flowers for use by people.

INTRODUCTION
RoboBee!

Words to Understand

algorithms   problem-solving computer programs

autonomous   independent; self-directed

etymologists   scientists who study insects

forage   search for; usually, as in looking for food

vortex   spinning air

No insect is as important to farming as the buzzing honeybee. Not only do the tiny insects produce sweet-tasting honey, but they also pollinate 80 percent of all flowering crops, or nearly 33 percent of everything we eat. In the United States alone, honeybees pollinate about $24 billion worth of crops and produce $10 billion worth of honey each year.

Several years ago, beekeepers started to notice that honeybees were dying in huge numbers. **Etymologists** and others tried to figure out why. They concluded it was a phenomenon called Colony Collapse Disorder (CCD).

CCD occurs when nearly all the adult bees in a colony—except the queen—die out. No one knows why CCD happens, although some speculate it has to do with the bee's environment or tiny parasites that kill the bees from the inside out. Whatever the cause, one thing is certain: If the honeybee becomes extinct, most of the world's pollinated plants will also vanish.

Armed with this sober knowledge, researchers at Harvard University and Northeastern University in Massachusetts undertook a project to save the food supply by building robotic bees that might one day pollinate fields of crops. Known as RoboBees, the **autonomous** flying micro-bots have yet to take flight in any serious way. However, the tiny machines offer farmers the ability to turn agriculture on its ear.

Using electronic sensors and cameras instead of antennae and eyes, each diminutive RoboBee will one day buzz across fields of

This is RoboBee, shown in comparison to a small bolt. Yes, the tiny flying machine is that small. But it might someday be used to help farmers.

flowering crops adapting to changes in the environment. Moreover, they will be able to communicate with one another, just as real bees do when they scout and **forage** for food.

On the Fly

In creating the RoboBee, researchers had to study how real insects—namely the housefly—took flight. They also had to find out why some insects, like the honeybee, are able to work in groups. As they gained this knowledge, engineers began designing computer **algorithms** to mimic these and other behaviors. Eventually RoboBees will be able to use this software to coordinate simple tasks, such as where to fly and what flower on which to land.

"If you want to make something a centimeter big that can fly, several hundred thousand solutions already exist in nature," Robert Wood, an electrical engineer at Harvard's Microbotics Lab, told *National Geographic*. "We don't just copy nature. We try to understand the what, how, and why behind an organism's anatomy, movement, and behavior, and then translate that into engineering terms."

Flight of the RoboBee

In designing the RoboBee, scientists studied high-speed videos of insects in flight to understand how the bugs' wings worked. From these videos, scientists learned that as an insect's wings flap, a **vortex** of air, similar to a tornado, forms along the edge of the wing. The spinning causes air pressure to drop above the wings, while increasing air pressure below the wings. As that happens, air is pushed up, and the bug begins to fly.

To keep the bug moving through the air, the insect's wings rotate as it prepares to flap its wings in the opposite direction. That creates a force similar to backspin on a ping-pong ball. As that rotation occurs, it pulls a faster moving column of air over the top of the wing that strikes the swirling vortex created by the previous wing stroke, generating an additional upward or downward force.

RoboBees design poses
new challenges

Wood and his group have already developed a way to make and assemble the tiny machines. Each has a wingspan of only 1.2 inches (3 cm) and weighs 80 milligrams, or .0028 ounces. The RoboBees flap their wings 120 times a second and can hover and fly along paths that are already programmed into its electronic brain.

Although the ultimate goal of the research is to create swarms of robotic bugs that will move from flower to flower, Wood says the bots can be used for other purposes, too, such as tracking chemical spills, or helping to locate trapped survivors after a natural disaster.

March of Progress

Agriculture, the science and practice of farming, is central to our existence. Anything scientists can do to make the job easier has the ability to affect the entire planet. That's because the world's food supply is in peril as population increases and global climate change ruin the environment. To help battle these problems, scientists work every day to design new methods and tools, such as RoboBees, that farmers can use to help feed the planet. Currently, there are more than 7 billion of us in the world—a number that is expected to rise to 9 billion in another 40 years.

Food is already in such short supply in many areas that, according to the United Nations, 12 children die each minute because they cannot get enough to eat. Most live in poor developing countries such as those in Africa.

While much scientific research is focused on improving crop resistance to weeds, insects, and diseases, other researchers are finding new ways for farmers to use computers, global positioning systems, and other technologies to save water, seed, fuel, and fertilizers.

The science of farming is growing every day.

 Text-Dependent Questions

1. Why is the honeybee important to agriculture?

2. What is Colony Collapse Disorder?

3. How many people are there in the world today?

 Research Project

Use the library and the Internet to research where early humans first began to farm. Plot these locations on a map. What can you conclude about the areas in which farming took place? What are the similarities? Research further to understand how farming helped spread civilization. Which civilizations thrived in the areas you plotted on the map?

Everyone is familiar with the use of cows for meat and dairy products. But scientists are finding new and remarkable uses for what comes out of cows.

SCIENCE AND
Agriculture

Words to Understand

antimicrobial   describing a substance that kills or limits the growth microorganisms

ecosystem   a collection of all living things in a particular environment

glucose   sugar in plants that is used as food for energy

pathogens   something, such as a virus or a bacterium, that can cause a disease

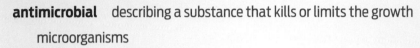

Some agricultural scientists spend their days studying farm animals, crops, or diseases. Others want to know how insects and weather conditions affect the growth of plants. Still others work to develop new mechanical tools to make farming easier.

Tim McAllister studies cow dung.

Specifically, McAllister, a research scientist in Canada, is interested in finding the best ways to control bacteria that live in the animal's poop. A single cow can expel up to 120 pounds (54 kg) of manure a day. Farmers often use the animal waste as an inex-

When cow dung is stacked in piles like these, the built-in heat of the manure slowly rises toward bacteria-killing temperatures. It makes the dung useful as fertilizer.

pensive source of fertilizers, which are nutrient-rich compounds that help crops grow.

Yet, cow dung presents farmers with several problems—besides its smell. For one thing, fresh cow manure can contain harmful bacteria, such as *E. coli*, *Salmonella*, and *Yesinia*, all of which can make people and animals extremely sick. In order to keep everyone healthy, farmers inject or feed their cattle **antimicrobial** drugs that kill the tiny organisms—sometimes.

However, certain types of bacteria have reengineered their genes to resist these powerful medicines. Sometimes these drug-resistant bacteria exchange their DNA with other bacteria that can cause human infections. DNA is short for deoxyribonucleic acid, a spiral-shaped molecule of chemicals that contain the genes, or inherited characteristics, of a living organism. When a cow defecates or urinates, the disease-resistant bugs and their DNA can also enter the **ecosystem**.

"When you use antibiotics, bacterial resistance is inevitable," McAllister told a reporter for Science Daily. "There's always trade-offs in nature. It really is a matter of which bacteria become resistant and if it has any implications for human health."

Fortunately, bacteria (even those that resist antimicrobial drugs) cannot survive in high temperatures, which is why farmers "cook" the manure before applying dung as fertilizer.

Don't get grossed out. Farmers don't bake the dung in an oven or over a grill. Instead, they heap mounds of fresh cow manure in pyramid-shape piles. The dung piles act like an oven, heating up to temperatures of more than 131°F (55°C) in just a few days. As the dung pile gets hotter, bacteria die.

A look back at the first farmers

Another way to cook and kill bacteria is to spread manure in long rows and keep churning the dung from top to bottom as if you were mixing cake batter.

McAllister wanted to know which method—piling or stirring—was the best way to kill bacteria and degrade the DNA associated with antibiotic resistance. To that end, McAllister took manure from cattle treated with antibiotics and let some of it sit in piles. He churned up the rest.

Frogs are right at home in algae-covered ponds, but scientists are looking into growing and farming the prolific plant for use as human food.

McAllister found that while piling dung in huge piles killed some antibiotic-resistant bacteria, it wasn't thorough enough. Most of the heat was concentrated in the middle of the piles and did not reach the edges. Mixing the dung in long rows was more effective. McAllister says churning increased the temperature of the dung rows to a deadly 160°F (71°C).

Pond Scum Rules

Tim McAllister studies cow dung. Alistair McCormick studies pond scum. While the green slime, also known as algae, is not a human food crop, it holds important information that might one day help farmers increase wheat, rice, and barley production.

Superbug on the Loose

Scientists announced in 2015 that they had discovered a gene in *E. coli* that makes the deadly bug resistant to one of the strongest antibiotics in the world. Moreover, the gene can also transfer itself to other **pathogens**, such as *Pseudomonas aeruginosa*, which can infect animals, plants, and humans. Right now, the gene, which scientists found on a pig farm, is confined to China. Yet, they fear it eventually will spread around the world.

Working at the University of Edinburgh's School of Biological Sciences in Great Britain, McCormick became interested in why green algae grows and spreads like no one's business. He found the cells in algae absorbed more carbon dioxide (CO_2) during photosynthesis than other plants. Photosynthesis is the process by which plants use the sun's light to turn water and carbon dioxide into oxygen and **glucose**.

Because algae have special mechanisms in their cells that boost carbon levels, they are able to produce more glucose, which means they are able to multiply faster than other plants. Most food crops, such as vegetables and grains, cannot raise their concentration of CO2 in the same way. McCormick wondered if he could manipulate the cells in these crops to mimic algae's photosynthetic process.

McCormick went to work studying the cells of algae to understand which parts played a role in photosynthesis. When he found those components, he extracted and then transferred them to plants that were more complex. His experiment was a success. The algae's cell parts took hold in the cells of the new plants. McCormick's next step is to find a way to use that process to increase the production of crops, especially wheat and other grains.

"Simple plants such as algae are very good at fixing carbon from the air, compared with complex plants such as rice and wheat," McCormick told a science reporter. "If we can harness the systems that simple plants use to grow efficiently, we may be able to create highly productive crops."

Farming in Space

In 2015, astronauts aboard the International Space Station did something amazing—they ate a salad of red romaine lettuce. This was no ordinary feast, however. It was the first meal that humans had consumed with food grown in outer space.

Although the lettuce wasn't the first crop grown in outer space (other foods have been grown in space before but were brought back to Earth for testing), it was an important milestone. If humans are to spend any significant time away from Earth, they will have to grow food crops to survive. Not only will humans be able eat

Aboard the International Space Station, U.S. astronaut Steve Swanson harvests a crop of red romaine lettuce that the station crew grew in the zero gravity of space.

space crops, but the plants can help remove toxic carbon dioxide from air inside a spacecraft, while expelling life-giving oxygen.

Yet, growing a plant in outer space is not as simple as it is on Earth. Here on Earth, the roots of plants grow downward because gravity—the force of attraction between objects—is pulling them in that direction.

Inside the roots are special cells called *stratocytes*. Inside these cells are tiny structures known as *statoliths*. When Earth's gravity tugs on the statoliths, the structures sink to the bottom of the cells. That forces the plant's roots to grow downward. In space, however, there is little gravity to pull on the statoliths, which is

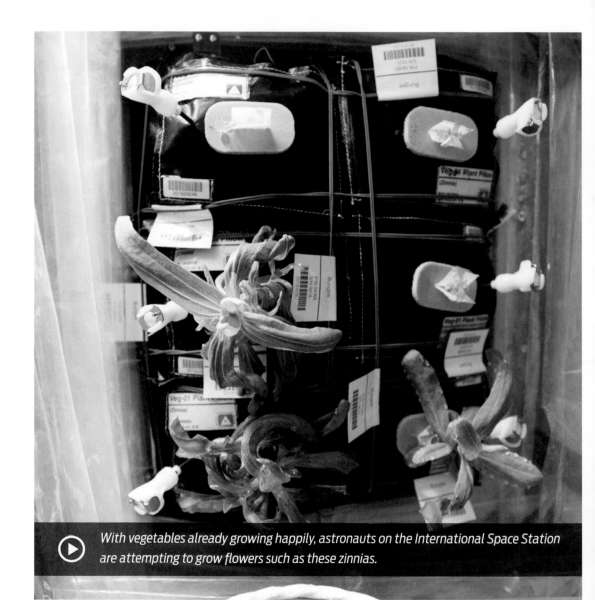

With vegetables already growing happily, astronauts on the International Space Station are attempting to grow flowers such as these zinnias.

why scientists have to find different ways for different plants to take root.

Lack of sunlight is another problem. Sunlight is abundant on Earth and is an important part of photosynthesis, the process by which plants create the carbohydrates that they need to grow. Space is mostly dark. As a result, scientists have to develop light systems that help the plants grow.

Benefits for Farmers

As scientists work out solutions for these and other problems, they have taken what they have already learned to make farming on Earth more productive. For example, when plants grow, whether on Earth or in outer space, they give off a gas called ethylene, which ripens fruits and vegetables. It also speeds up their decay.

To get around this problem, scientists developed an ethylene scrubbing system that can cleanse the air of the chemical. As a result, fruits and vegetables last longer.

Researchers also invented a leaf sensor that measures how thirsty a plant is. Water is scarce in space, so a space farmer will have to conserve water on a long space flight. The sensor measures leaf thickness, which corresponds to the amount of moisture inside the plant. When the moisture content drops to a certain level, the sensor lets the astronaut know that it is time to water. Farmers on Earth use the sensors, too. The sensors send a text message that lets the farmer know when it is time to irrigate the crops. The sensors are a great way to save water, especially in dry areas.

Frankenfish

Genetically modified organisms (GMO), in which scientists alter a plant's DNA to give it new characteristics, have been around for a while. In fact, there are 448 million acres (181.3 million hectares) of genetically modified crops growing in the world today.

Yet, there aren't too many genetically modified animals on our dinner table. That will soon change. In November 2015, the U.S. Food and Drug Administration (FDA), the federal agency that makes sure our medicines and foods are safe, said it was okay for aqua farmers to begin producing and selling a genetically altered Atlantic salmon. Aqua farmers raise fish and other aquatic life as sources of food.

Scientists altered the salmon's DNA so it would grow faster than any other salmon. Scientists created the "super salmon" by taking a gene that regulates the growth of a Chinook salmon and inserting it into the genes of an Atlantic salmon. The result was a fast-growing fish.

The FDA said scientific studies "demonstrated that the inserted genes remained stable over several generations of fish, that food from the [genetically engineered] salmon is safe to eat by humans and animals, that the genetic engineering is safe for the fish, and the salmon meets the sponsor's claim about faster growth."

Some people say genetically modified foods, which they call "Frankenfoods" after the classic horror tale *Frankenstein*, might harm people, plants, and the environment. After reviewing all the studies, the FDA decided that wasn't the case with the salmon. Officials said the genetically altered salmon would not impact the environment in any significant way. For one thing, the salmon will be bred in special pens preventing the creatures from entering the ecosystem and establishing themselves in the wild.

The fish will not be produced in the United States, but at two aqua farms in Canada and Panama, a country in Central America. Moreover, the company that altered the fish said they would only grow female salmon so the fish cannot reproduce.

The small salmon grew in nature; the large salmon grew with the help of science. Genetically modified animals have potential to increase food supplies.

GMO Foods

GMO foods are modified for a variety of reasons. Some are altered to tolerate herbicides better than non-GMO crops. That means farmers can use the poisons to control weeds without harming their GMO crops.

Other foods are engineered to cut down on the amount of poisonous pesticides farmers spray on their crops to kill insects. These foods contain a gene from a common soil bacterium called Bacillus thuringiensis, or BT for short. The bacterium makes its own pesticide, a toxic protein that kills insects but doesn't harm the plant or people. You cannot taste the difference between GMO food and regular food.

Bug Out

Aren't ladybugs sweet? They are colorful, and they don't bite you. Heck, no one ever stomps on a ladybug, or at least they shouldn't. Yet, ladybugs are killers, which is why many farmers love them. Ladybugs like to chow down on crop-destroying pests like aphids and mites. Some scientists believe these colorful killers will one day take the place of pesticides.

In Japan, researchers bred a family of non-flying ladybugs that farmers can use as a nonchemical "biopesticide." Tomokazu Seko, a researcher from the National Agriculture and Food Research Organization in Fukuyama, Japan, bred 30 generations of one species of ladybug, *Harmonia axyridis*, until he came up with one that stayed on a plant and ate other bugs. Once Seko made the discovery, the bug was put to use. It reduced the damage to Japan's mustard spinach crop by 90 percent.

Japanese researchers are breeding new types of ladybugs that can be "aimed" directly at a particular pest on a particular type of plant.

 # Text-Dependent Questions

1. How many pounds of manure can a cow expel each day?

2. Explain the process and importance of photosynthesis.

3. What are stratocytes and statoliths?

 # Research Project

As genetically modified foods become more available, there has been a lot of discussion on whether the products should be clearly labeled. Break off into two groups of four and five, research the pros and cons of labeling genetically modified food, and hold a debate.

Sensors attached to equipment out in the fields—such as field-swarming combines—now helps farmers to better gauge the health of their crops—and their profits!

TECHNOLOGY AND
Agriculture

2

In Leesburg, Indiana, Kip Tom is a seventh-generation farmer who tries to squeeze as much profit from his corn and soybean fields as he can. To do that, he attaches sensors to tractors and harvesters to gauge the yield of his fields and the health of his crops. He irrigates his plants using a smartphone app.

In Texas, Brian Braswell relies on orbiting satellites to plow fields with such amazing accuracy that there is only an inch between furrows. When he's not sowing seeds, Braswell sprays his fields with exact amounts of fertilizer that is surgically dispensed by a computer. In Nevada, Iowa, Ken Blackledge hopes to one day use a robot to weed fields, saving him time, money, and energy.

All three are part of a growing community of farmers that is relying less on muscle power and more on technology to increase production and keep costs down. "I'm hooked on a drug of information and productivity," Kip Tom told *The New York Times*. "Farmers still think tech means…more horsepower, more fertilizer. They don't see that technology…is about multiplying information."

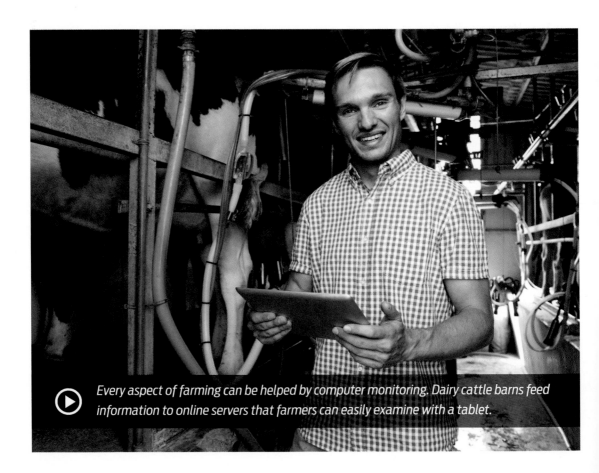

Every aspect of farming can be helped by computer monitoring. Dairy cattle barns feed information to online servers that farmers can easily examine with a tablet.

Although new machines and farming techniques have made farming easier and more profitable over the years, most farmers still plow, plant, and harvest crops in the same tedious and muscle-aching way—by hand. Despite all the advances made over 12,000 years, drought, blight, or a leaf-eating insect can still wreck fields and force farmers to lose money.

To combat these and other agricultural miseries, tractors, combines, and other machines are now armed with an array of devices that can test soil, map fields, and track the health of individual plants. Some farmers, for example, use high-resolution satellite images delivered directly to a tablet or laptop to tell them whether crops are healthy or if a fungus is creeping over the fields.

Others use satellites that can measure the **chlorophyll** content of plants, allowing farmers to assess how hearty their plants are. "It used to be, if you could turn a wrench you'd be good at farming," one farmer told *The New York Times*. "Now you need to know screen navigation, and pinpointing what data should go where so people can plan and predict."

Flight of the Drones

Perhaps no one technology has the ability to revolutionize farming more than robotic drones, also known as unmanned aerial vehicles (UAVs). Although most people think of drones as weapons of war, agriculture drones will make up at least 80 percent of the future commercial market, according to the Association for Unmanned Vehicle Systems International. Experts say drones will be as important to farming in the 21st century as the steam engine was in the 19th century.

UAVs will give farmers the ability to treat specific areas with pesticides and herbicides, reducing costs and the amount of chemicals farmers use. Drones will also be deployed as worker bees, such as the RoboBee, to pollinate fields. The remote-controlled vehicles will also be able to use high-resolution cameras to help farmers target where the next load of fertilizer should be sprayed, or which crops need watering. The UAVs will

Remote-controlled drones, or UAVs, are already being used by farmers to map their lands, photograph growth, and plan future plantings.

also be able to spot diseases earlier and look for signs of drought.

Experts say drones will cut costs for farmers, allowing them to increase production and reap more profit. Drones will also help the environment by reducing the amount of pesticides, herbicides, and chemical fertilizers. According to the American Farm Bureau Federation, drones can help soybean and wheat farmers increase yields and profits.

'Bots on the Ground

Not only will robotic aircraft fly over fields, but researchers are also building an army of ground-based robots that will do a variety of chores. The machines collect water samples and figure out when apple and peach trees need to be pruned. Some robots will be able to count individual plants and see what bugs or fungi might be attacking them.

Farming Through Text Messages

While the digital technology that allows drones to fly and combines to harvest crops more efficiently is expensive, farmers in many areas, especially those in developing nations, are using a less complicated form of technology to better their lives.

Small-scale farmers in several African nations use cell phones to track weather, rainfall, and seed prices. The cell phone gives these farmers an edge because most do not have the right training or resources to allow them to move beyond subsistence farming. Often, their crops fail because of drought, pests, and disease.

SMS technology, or "Short Message Service," allows farmers to text one another to share information and solve problems. One mobile technology, for example, sends texts to farmers on how to combat pest problems and prevent infection among farm animals.

Synthetic Meat

For many people, there's nothing more mouth-watering than the smell of bacon frying on the stove, or a juicy steak sizzling on a backyard grill. Yet, whether it is a pig, a cow, or a chicken, meat gets to your table in the same way: the animals are raised on factory-like farms and killed in slaughterhouses. Butchers then carve and package the meat for sale.

To satisfy the world's appetite for meat and meat products, including dairy, eggs, and leather goods, farmers maintain a herd of about 60 billion animals. By 2050, that number will need to increase to 100 billion to accommodate the world's growing population.

Such growth will take a huge toll on the environment as farmers use more land, more water, and more feed to raise the animals. Currently, 70 percent of agricultural land and 8 percent of the global water supply is devoted to livestock production.

Since the growth of livestock is seemingly **unsustainable**, scientists believe they have found the answer to the problem—a technology called biofabrication. Biofabrication is the creation of a product using stem cells. Stem cells are so-called master cells that have the ability to morph into tissue-specific cells.

The public got its first glimpse at how biofabrication works when a group of diners ate a hamburger on a Monday afternoon in the Netherlands in 2013. The burger was a bit dry and lacked flavor. However, it was an amazing piece of meat because it did

Hamburger or not hamburger? The end result is mostly the same, but the origin is quite different. This product is not from a cow, but was grown in a lab.

not come from a cow. Instead, it was made in a laboratory test tube using bovine stem cells. Scientists extracted the cells from a cow's shoulder and put them in a petri dish where they swam in a nutrient-rich solution.

Over time, the cells multiplied, eventually becoming strips of bovine muscle tissue. Scientists used about 20,000 of these strips to make a five-ounce burger, which also contained bread crumbs, salt, and natural colorings. The meat did not contain any fat. Scientists served up the burger, which cost $300,000 to make, on a bun with lettuce and tomato slices.

Josh Schonwald told *The New York Times* that the bite he took felt "like a conventional hamburger" and tasted "like an animal-protein cake."

Biofabrication is already used in medicine as scientists use human stem cells to grow various body parts such as ears, skin, blood vessels, and bones. Although biofabricated food might sound like a recipe out of a futuristic cookbook, it is nothing new. Humans have been manufacturing products using cell cultures for thousands of years, including wine, beer, and yogurt.

High in protein, easily grown at a low cost, and available in many varieties, insects are seen by some experts as a significant food source in the future.

Scientists say that biofabricated meat will not only increase the food supply, but it will stop the slaughter of animals for food. All the animals would have to do is donate a few stems cells so that scientists can grow them into a veal chop, a chicken leg, or a strip steak.

Insect Farms

Eating a slice of beef grown in a test tube is one thing. But would you eat a piece of meat if the animal was fed a diet of maggots?

Sounds nauseating, but it is already happening. As Earth's population grows and the demand for meat increases, farmers are using more feed to keep their herds alive before the slaughter. In fact, the United Nations Food and Agricultural Organization said farmers will need 70 percent more feed just for cattle by 2050. Moreover, a third of livestock feed comes from dwindling fish supplies.

The impact on the environment will be staggering as farmers use more **arable** land to grow livestock feed. But some farmers have a solution—they feed their livestock maggots. In case you might have forgotten, maggots are fly larvae. They feast on

Greenhouse Animal

Domestic livestock, such as cattle, buffalo, sheep, and goats are the largest producers of greenhouse gases, producing up to 50 percent of all emissions that drive global warming. All produce large amounts of methane, a greenhouse gas, as part of their normal digestive process. Methane also enters the environment when the animals' waste is stored in lagoons or holding tanks.

In addition, when thousands of animals congregate in one place, they create a biological breeding ground for disease, such as swine and avian flu.

Corn as Fuel

Corn ethanol is our most plentiful biofuel, yet it is not efficient to produce. If refineries turned every ear of corn into ethanol, it would replace only 12 percent of the gasoline supply. Moreover, the growing and manufacturing process that turns corn into ethanol produces only 15 percent less greenhouse gas than gasoline.

decomposing tissue such as vegetable peelings, pig intestines, and other biodegradable waste.

A South African company opened the first "fly farm" in 2015. The flies deposit their eggs on rotting waste products. Once the maggots hatch, they feed for several days before workers harvest them. The bugs are then washed, dried, milled, packaged, and sold as livestock feed, providing farmers with an alternative to other livestock feed, such as grains, fishmeal, and soybeans.

Food as Fuel

Some crops are grown as food. Other crops, however, are grown as a source of fuel. The process of turning food crops, such as corn, into **ethanol** that can power our vehicles, is very expensive. That's because cellulose, the most abundant naturally occurring organic molecule on the planet, is tough to break down and turn into alcohol. Cellulose is found in the cell walls of plants. Cows, goats, and deer and even termites can break cellulose molecules down without a problem because all have a gut full of bacteria and other microorganisms that can do the job efficiently.

In the laboratory, however, breaking down cellulose and turning it into a cost-effective fuel is much tougher. But that's not stopping scientists at Michigan State University from trying to turn the tough shell of cellulose into a usable alternative fuel. Researchers have developed a strain of corn that contains special enzymes that can turn stubborn cellulose into sugar. Engineers can then take that sugar and ferment it into ethanol. Other scientists are trying to build a super microbe that can do the job on an industrial scale, which will bring the cost of ethanol-based fuels down.

Text-Dependent Questions

1. What are UAVs and how will farmers use them?

2. How much agricultural land is devoted to livestock production?

3. What are stem cells and why are they important?

Research Project

Research which food crops can be used to create alternative biofuel sources. Write a report comparing each crop. When writing, consider these questions: Which food crops are viable sources of alternative energy? Which are the most (and least) expensive to create? How does the growth of biofuel crops affect their use as food crops?

In dark Underground tunnels deep beneath London's famous Big Ben, a revolutionary new site for agriculture is growing crops in an environment that might point the way to the future in farming.

ENGINEERING AND
Agriculture

Words to Understand

desertification   the process by which land becomes increasingly arid, or dry

infrared   a portion of invisible light in the electromagnetic spectrum between visible light and radio waves

translucent   a clear material that allows light to pass through

ultraviolet   relating to light which humans cannot see; its waves are shorter than visible light, but longer than X-rays

Below the streets of London, in an underground World War II air raid shelter that once protected Britons from German bombs, sits a garden of radish, celery, and spinach shoots. As one would expect from such an underground tunnel, there is no soil and no sunlight, two things the plants need to grow and thrive.

Yet, they do just that thanks to two engineers who are experimenting with a new way to increase the world's food supply without using what's left of Earth's arable land—that portion of

By growing plants underground, scientists are exploring ways to expand food production without having a negative impact on the ever-shrinking land aboveground.

the planet that farmers use to grow crops. Although Steve Dring and Richard Ballard know underground farms will never feed the world's population by themselves, the idea of growing food crops where they don't usually grow intrigues them and others as traditional farmland dwindles. In the future, will your vegetables come from caves and rooms carved out around the subways and underground railroads near you?

The Not-So-Good Earth

Although Earth is huge, there isn't a lot of land on which farmers can grow food. For one thing, 75 percent of Earth is water, while half of the remaining 25 percent is desert or frozen. That leaves about one-eighth of the planet suitable for farming. Humans, however, have paved over most of that land for roads, towns, villages, and cities. That means roughly 1/32nd of Earth's surface can be used for agriculture.

Yet, even that amount is shrinking. Human activities along with climate change are slowly turning once productive fields into dry wasteland. It's a process called **desertification**. During desertification, fragile topsoil can be washed or blown away by wind and rain. Poor farming practices, including robbing the soil of nutrients and overgrazing grassland with livestock, along with the destruction of forests and grasslands by humans, all contribute to the problem.

According to the United Nations, desertification affects an estimated 25 to 30 percent of the world's land surface. That is why many people, including Dring and Ballard, believe that finding new places to cultivate is essential for humanity.

An Underground Greenhouse

It's not easy to grow crops underground where the sun never shines and rain never falls. Yet, Dring and Ballard were able to accomplish the amazing feat by using hydroponics, a system that cultivates plants without the use of soil.

The two men engineered a system that allows water to circulate through a series of trays that hold the plants. Instead of using soil, the men took old carpets from hotel rooms, which proved to be a perfect medium for the plants to take root. The partners also strung together a series of LED lights powered by wind turbines on the surface. The lights emit both **ultraviolet** and **infrared** light that the plants soak up to assist in photosynthesis. The lights are on for 18 hours a day, while huge fans keep the temperature of the tunnel at 69°F (21°C), a most comfortable temperature for growing vegetables. Dring and Ballard can usually harvest the crops within 6 to 28 days, depending on the plant.

"We're not planning to take over traditional farming," Dring told *National Geographic*. "But we are trying to confront the idea that we're running out of land and need to find new places to produce food."

Rooftop Farms

You wouldn't think that among the skyscrapers, bridges, and bright lights of New York City you'd find a large farm. Yet, one does exist. The farm is not located in Central Park, or along the Hudson River. Instead, it sits atop two roofs in the borough of Brooklyn, not far from where baseball's old Brooklyn Dodgers once played. (They moved to a more a fertile field in Los Angeles in 1958.)

Known as the Brooklyn Grange, the 2.5-acre (1 hectare) farm is the largest rooftop farm in the world, growing more than 50,000

While Brooklyn is the main focus of large-scale rooftop gardening in New York City, smaller, private plots such as this one in Manhattan are using every inch of space.

pounds (22,679 kg) of vegetables and herbs each year. The farmers sell their rooftop bounty to local restaurants and food markets.

Still, Brooklyn Grange is not the only rooftop farm in the Big Apple. A few miles away in the South Bronx, engineers are planning to build an even larger garden. This one will cover 200,000 square feet (185 sq m) atop an old warehouse located at the southeastern edge of the East River, in the middle of several food distribution businesses. Other rooftop farms are also thriving throughout the city.

New York is not the only urban area to embrace rooftop farming. From St. Louis to Milwaukee to London to Singapore, rooftop

Some restaurants in New York City and other large cities are planting rooftop gardens to provide a ready supply of organic greens for salads.

farms are sprouting all around the world, transforming concrete jungles into fertile fields. Experts say these once-wasted spaces have the ability to transform agriculture as arable land disappears. According to the U.S. Department of Agriculture, about 15 percent of the world's food is grown in cities.

A closer look at rooftop farming

Rooftop farms come in all shapes and sizes. In Singapore, for example, plants grow in rows of pipe that are stacked on top of one another. The plants sprout through tiny holes in the pipe as nutrient-rich water passes underneath. The water comes from the building's plumbing system, but before it reaches the plants, it first must pass through large fish tanks of tilapia. The waste excreted by the fish is rich in nutrients, which allows the plants to thrive. The keepers of the farm harvest and sell the tilapia when they mature.

More Than Just a Farm

Rooftop farms not only provide people with food, but they are also engineered to help the environment. One way rooftop farms do this is by reducing a form of energy called the urban heat island, or UHI. Urban heat islands are cities in which the temperature is significantly warmer than the surrounding countryside.

The phenomenon occurs when the surfaces that make up a city, such as concrete, blacktop, and steel, soak up the sun's energy. These surfaces absorb heat during the day, and release it when the sun goes down at night. This creates an unnatural warming effect, which ultimately increases the amount of energy people use to cool homes and businesses.

By planting rows of crops on rooftops, the temperature of the surrounding air becomes cooler, reducing the effects of the urban heat island. In fact, a number of roof farms located in the same Boston neighborhood have decreased the amount of energy used by residents to cool their homes.

Most roof farms are also engineered to take advantage of storm water runoff. When it rains, roof farms slow the amount of water coming off a building, which reduces pollution of local waterways.

Other Challenges

Although rooftop farms have many benefits, they also provide engineers with a number of challenges, such as whether the building underneath the farm can withstand hundreds of thousands of pounds of soil and water.

To get around this problem, engineers have found many ways to distribute the weight of the roof farm more effectively. One stabilizing process uses steel stilts that transfer the weight of the farm to a building's load-bearing walls. Some roof farms also use hydroponic trays, which decrease the overall weight of the farm.

Since some rooftop farms are giant greenhouses, they have to be built to withstand storms and blowing wind. One rooftop greenhouse design utilizes a giant sail of **translucent** fabric stretched over curved ribs of steel that deflects wind as it blows.

Other rooftop farms are built to share energy, air, and water with the building underneath. In some buildings, garden-fresh breezes blow from the farm through the building, increasing the amount of oxygen in the air. (Plants exhale oxygen, while breathing in carbon dioxide, in a process called respiration.) Some farms also recycle wastewater from sinks, bathtubs, and drinking fountains.

Water woes: Causes and effects

The dry areas of the Nevada desert depend on ever-shrinking streams like this one to provide irrigation for farms.

Water Woes

Finding more space to grow food is fine, but it doesn't matter if there is little water to irrigate crops. The people of Moapa Valley, Nevada, know this firsthand.

▶ *The stark white lower walls around Lake Mead are a clear indication of how low the water levels have fallen as parts of the West deal with ongoing drought.*

Located an hour away from the glittering lights and casinos of Las Vegas, Moapa Valley is not as fertile as it once was. Years ago, the valley was a cornucopia of fruits, vegetables, eggs, and honey. Farmers irrigated their fields with water from the Muddy River, which flows into the Colorado River.

Today, the valley is a patchwork of mostly brown fields. There are many reasons for this change. For one thing, the valley receives only five inches of rain a year—barely enough to fill a good-sized coffee mug. Another part of the problem is that Las Vegas is an expanding city. As the city grows outward, it buys more farmland and the water associated with that land. As a result, local farmers, such as those in Moapa Valley, have less water to irrigate their crops.

Another part of the equation is that the main source of water for Las Vegas is drying up because of a terrible drought that has lasted more than a decade. The city gets most of its water from the Colorado River and its tributaries, including the Muddy River. All that water is penned up in Lake Mead, which sits behind Hoover Dam. The water level of Lake Mead, once the largest reservoir in the United States, has dropped nearly 100 feet (30 m) within the past 10 years.

Evidence of the drought can be seen in the "bathtub ring," the lake's high-water mark whitewashed by minerals in the water. Experts say things will get worse before they get better as the region's population increases and climate change worsens. Yet, such dire predictions have not stopped engineers from trying to find ways to get farmers and others the water they need.

A Boring Machine

The tunneling machine that bored the three-mile tunnel under Lake Mead is a technological marvel. Powered by electric motors, the machine had the power of 7,700 horses. On the front of the machine was a high-speed grinder that used disks to grind up against the rock, breaking it into small pieces. Scoops on the cutter head dropped the pulverized rock onto a conveyer belt that spat the rock out of the back of the machine, where workers then carted it away.

One of the most ambitious projects was to build a pipeline under Lake Mead to ensure that the region would still have enough water if the water level falls below the mouth of two huge intake pipes. In 2015, workers finished the seven-year tunneling project. They hollowed out a three-mile tunnel 600 feet (183 m) below the lake using a specially designed tunneling machine. The machine chewed up the rocks and spit them back out.

As workers cleared the rock, they installed ringed segments that they then pieced together to form the inside of the tunnel pipe. Working 24 hours a day, engineers then connected the tunnel to a third intake pipe, which will draw water from the lake if the water level gets too low.

This was not an easy engineering project. The tunnel flooded twice, delaying the project and forcing engineers to find another route. One person also died. The project had a price tag of $800 million.

Desalination

Another way for farmers to obtain water is to tap into the ocean, a process called desalination. Ocean water is salty and cannot be used for cooking, drinking, or watering crops. However, desalination transforms salt water into freshwater.

In 2014, engineers in Mexico and in San Diego County, California, began building a large desalination plant in Mexico that will transform 100 million gallons (378 million l) of seawater a day into freshwater. Engineers also built a desalination plant in Baja, Mexico, that produces 5.7 million gallons (21.6 million l) of water a day. As of 2014, 15 desalination projects were moving forward in water-starved California, the largest of which is scheduled to go online in 2016 near Carlsbad.

When building desalination plants, engineers install intake pipes that pump millions of gallons of water from the sea. As the water passes through the system, special filters remove sediment,

Osmosis tubes such as these are used in desalination plants. The saltwater flows around and around, as each filter removes more and more of the salt to end with freshwater.

Using desalination is a balancing act between taking water from the sea and making sure that the salt that goes back in does not disturb delicate ecosystems.

bacteria, and viruses. Once that process is completed, the ocean water is pumped through another series of filters that removes the salt. The freshwater is then purified, stored, and delivered.

Figuring out what to do with the wastewater from the desalination plants is always a major challenge for engineers because the process produces wastewater that is saltier than seawater. Engineers need to return the water to the ocean, but it cannot be saltier than what is already there. More salt would disrupt the ocean's ecosystem. Before the wastewater is returned to the ocean, workers have to mix the wastewater with less salty seawater, which cuts down on the amount of salt returning to the ocean.

 ## Text-Dependent Questions

1. How much of Earth's surface can be used for agriculture?

2. Describe how an urban heat island works.

3. How far has the level of Lake Mead dropped in the past decade?

 ## Research Project

Create a public service poster or computer slideshow presentation highlighting the effects of climate change on the world's food supply. Make sure you use pictures and statistics to create a compelling presentation. If you wish, you can make the presentation local to your community or state.

Agricultural scientists depend on math for more than just counting up how much yield a particular field creates. Math models are a key tool in making sure that there is enough food for the world.

MATH AND
Agriculture

Words to Understand

consecutive   following one after the other

erosion   gradual wearing away of the land

habitats   the natural environments in which animals and plants live

ratios   relative relationships between two different numbers or quantities

Math has always been central to agriculture. Ancient farmers learned the importance of numbers early on, as they had to figure out ways to measure out enough seed for the next year's harvest. They also had to measure time accurately so they knew when to plant and when to harvest.

As farming grew, math became increasingly important. No longer were farmers just growing food for their own use. They also sold and traded whatever surplus they had. Farming quickly became a business, and successful businesses are those that are profitable. To become profitable, farmers have to find ways to increase production of their crops and control expenses. They couldn't do it without math.

Farmers use math to figure finances and calculate fertilizer and herbicide rates. Farmers also use math to measure the capacity of grain silos and to determine crop yields. The list seems endless.

Precise math not only allows a farm to thrive, but it can also help the environment. Here are a few examples.

Calculating Soil Erosion

Combating soil **erosion** is one of the most important ways farmers use math. When farmers plow their fields, the exposed topsoil can be blown away by wind or washed away by rain. In Brazil, for example, 55 million tons of topsoil are washed away each year when farmers plant crops of soy, coffee, cotton, corn, and tobacco. Water carries the soil into rivers, lakes, and coastal areas, damaging freshwater and marine **habitats**.

Figuring out how much soil erodes is based on a number of factors, including the type of soil being worn away, rainfall amounts, the velocity of raindrops, and the energy of storms. For example, a drizzle of rain will not erode as much land as a violent summer thunderstorm or a hurricane. To calculate soil loss due to erosion, scientists and farmers use a simple multiplication equation:

$$A = R \times K \times LS \times C \times P$$

Huge areas of Brazil are affected by erosion caused by the massive Amazon system, but man has created problems, too, with vast overcutting of forest land.

Where:

- A = annual tonnage of soil loss each year;
- R = the amount of erosion caused by total rainfall and its intensity;
- K = the ability of the soil to erode depending on its texture, the amount of organic material (living or dead roots) in the soil, and the soil's basic structure, such as soil with rounded surfaces versus blocky, cube-like flat surfaces;
- LS = the length and steepness of the land's slope;
- C = the types of crops grown;
- P = control practices farmers use, such as terracing and subsurface drainage.

By using this equation, agricultural scientists can take steps to limit erosion and decrease the amount of arable land that is destroyed. They can also help in minimizing the impact of toxic runoff into rivers, lakes, and streams caused by fertilizers and herbicides. Scientists can also minimize the impact of flooding.

Pest Control

Protecting crops is the foremost concern of all farmers. If a pest, for example, devastates a field of crops, the financial impact can be tremendous. Many farmers have lost their livelihood because of insects, fungi, and weeds.

The European corn borer is one of the most dangerous invasive pests that farmers in the United States and Canada are battling.

One of the most insidious pests is the moth-like European corn borer. Farmers first identified the bug in 1917. An immigrant from Europe, the corn borer came to the United States after hitching a ride on corn imported from Hungary and Italy. Since then, it has been the enemy of corn farmers in the eastern United States and Canada. The cost of controlling the corn borer and the damage it causes is roughly $1 billion a year.

Before deciding whether to treat corn fields with a pesticide to kill the pest, farmers have to figure out whether it is worth the expense. To do that, they have to calculate the number of corn borer larvae on each plant.

Doing the Math

Figuring out how much pesticide to mix and use is a tricky business. Farmers have a good understanding of **ratios** and fractions and are able to multiply correctly. For example, a pesticide maker says to apply three pounds (1.4 kg) of insecticide for every 1,000 square feet (93 sq m) of land. But a farmer has 10,000 square feet that needs to be treated. The farmer can figure out the correct amount to use by expressing this problem as a proportion.

Early planted corn is the most likely to develop a problem because the moths, which are looking for a place to hatch their eggs, are attracted to the tallest and greenest corn. Farmers will go out to their fields in June and early July and inspect 20 **consecutive** plants in each of five areas. They then count and record the number of plants that show corn borer damage.

Once that is accomplished, farmers need to determine whether it is worth the expense to get rid of the moths. They can use a special mathematical formula in deciding what to do. That formula takes into account several variables, including the number

The chewed-up ears of corn still on their stalks give ample evidence of the damage that corn borers and other pests can cause. These ears are wasted, thanks to pests.

of larvae found, the expected survivorship, the yield loss per acre, and the preventable loss per acre.

Here is an example of that formula at work if a farmer finds 450 corn borer larvae in 100 corn plants. The example is provided by the Department of Etymology at Iowa State University:

1. 450 larvae found   × 0.4 expected survivorship   = 180 surviving larvae

2. 180 surviving larvae   / 100 plants examined   = 1.8 larvae per plant

3. 1.8 larvae per plant   × 0.059 yield loss per larva   = 0.106 yield loss

4. 0.106 yield loss   × 140 expected yield (bushels per acre)   = 14.84 bushels loss per acre

5. 14.84 bushels loss per acre   × $2.50 price per bushel   = $37.10 loss per acre

6. $37.10 loss per acre   × 0.8 percent control   = $29.68 preventable loss/acre

7. $29.68 preventable loss/acre   − $14.00 cost of control per acre   = $15.68 profit (loss) per acre

From making robotic bees to engineering farms on rooftops, from creating GMO food to using math to help rid farms of pests, the aspects of STEM play a big part in making sure the world has enough food—today, and in the future.

 # Text-Dependent Questions

1. How does erosion occur?

2. Where did the corn borer originate?

3. What percentage of crops in the United States is lost to insect infestation today?

 # Research Project

Use this website **http://www.ipm.ucdavis.edu/EXOTIC/index.html#DISEASES** as a starting point to research the many pests that can destroy agricultural land. Pick one of the pests and research it further. Prepare an oral report on the insect and the damage it can do.

Find Out More

Books

Colson, Mary. *The Race to Feed the Hungry (World in Crisis)*. New York: Rosen Publishing Group, 2015.
Part of a series that explores how scientists and societies are seeking new ways to address world problems.

Conkin, Paul K. *A Revolution Down on the Farm: The Transformation of American Agriculture since 1929*. Lexington.: The University Press of Kentucky, 2008.
How modern farmers are keeping food on the table for a population that now numbers in the billions.

Miller, Debra A. *Organic Foods (Hot Topics)*. Farmington Hills, Mich.: Lucent Books, 2007.
The benefits and criticisms of the organic food movement, which has gone mainstream in recent years.

Websites

Iowa State University: Department of Entomology
https://www.ent.iastate.edu

Science Daily: Agriculture and Food
https://www.sciencedaily.com/news/plants_animals/agriculture_and_food/

UC Davis: Integrated Pest Management Program
http://www.ipm.ucdavis.edu/index.html

Series Glossary of Key Terms

capacity   the amount of a substance that an object can hold or transport

consumption   the act of using a product, such as electricity

electrodes   a material, often metal, that carries electrical current into or out of a nonmetallic substance

evaporate   to change from a liquid to a gas

fossil fuels   a fuel in the earth that formed long ago from dead plants and animals

inorganic   describing materials that do not contain the element carbon

intermittently   not happening in a regular or reliable way

ion   an atom or molecule containing an uneven number of electrons and protons, giving a substance either a positive or negative charge

microorganism   a tiny living creature visible only under a microscope

nuclear   referring to the nucleus, or center, of an atom, or the energy that can be produced by splitting or joining together atoms

organic   describing materials or life forms that contain the element carbon; all living things on Earth are organic

piston   part of an engine that moves up and down in a tube; its motion causes other parts to move

prototype   the first model of a device used for testing; it serves as a design for future models or a finished product

radiation   a form of energy found in nature that, in large quantities, can be harmful to living things

reactor   a device used to carry out a controlled process that creates nuclear energy

sustainable   able to be used without being completely used up, such as sunlight as an energy source

turbines   an engine with large blades that turn as liquids or gases pass over them

utility   a company chosen by a local government to provide an essential product, such as electricity

Index

Credits

About the Author

John Perritano is an award-winning journalist, writer, and editor from Southbury,
Conn., who has written numerous articles and books on a variety of subjects, includ-
ing science, sports, history, and culture for such publishers as National Geographic,
Scholastic, and Time/Life. His articles have appeared on Discovery.com, Popular
Mechanics.com, and other magazines and websites. He holds a master's degree in
American History from Western Connecticut State University.